A Dance in Melancholy

A collection of my articles, essays and memoirs

Homebound
Volume 1

I0426345

By

Q. M. Sidd

A Dance in Melancholy- Copyright © 2013 by Q. M. Sidd

Acknowledgement

I am thankful to God Almighty, above all, for his guidance without which a soul may roam but astray in the dark. I am undoubtedly indebted to my parents for their admirable encouragement that they have always bestowed upon me. I also wish to thank

I would also like to thank my Editor and a very good friend, Dr Hasan Gilani, an academic- a senior lecturer / Asst. Professor in the United Kingdom. With his PhD on Corporate Branding, Hasan has presented and published in several international conferences and is an associate editor of a few academic journals including International Journal of Knowledge Management and Journal of Change Management. I am indebted for his time and effort in editing my work.

To the spirit of mankind that breathes life in our deeds...

Contents

The Pakistan Challenge

The subject of Human Rights is as old as the history of mankind itself. It stretches back to the pre-historic times in to the medieval slavery era and journeys up to the present day. The world has evolved with time and people have learnt to fly and are reaching outer space yet the struggle for human rights is still on. If one reflects on this subject one finds oneself unfolding many stories of struggle with a human face. It reveals the struggles in the tales of people who fought for equality. William Wilberforce's struggle for abolition of the British slave trade as well as Martin Luther King's grandstand against racial discrimination are just a couple of instances whereas the journey continues in the shape of many untold stories. If we examine our world in retrospect; history is evident of this struggle. From the times of the Roman Empire in the west to the Ming China in the east- from the European Habsburg dynasty to the grand Ottoman empire- the story of human rights has its prints everywhere. And it does not even stop there but takes the history's path to the French revolution and encompasses the British colonial rule. Century after century the world saw wars and violations of human rights in the form of the clash of civilizations.

The biggest era of human rights violations was from the start till the mid of the 20th century when whole earth shattered and trembled with the two world wars resulting in the loss of millions of lives. The League of Nations and then afterwards the United Nations have been rendering their utmost to uphold the rights of the people through various legal and moral codes. However, the clash did not stop and we witnessed cold war and many conflicts enshrined therein. Now it all seems to have taken a new turn and this clash has drifted from boundaries to religion. Nonetheless, only to add to the misery alone, it is no longer the conflict of geographical civilizations alone but today we see it as a conflict amongst religious civilizations in the shape of terrorism and the war upon it. No matter which goggle one wears; it all revolves around deprivation of fundamental rights interwoven with a political enigma. It makes one wonder as to when it will stop. Will it stop? Will it bring long lasting peace if it ever did? These are only a few mind-baffling questions demanding vivid answers.

The Islamic Republic of Pakistan was created after the Second World War on 14ᵗʰ August 1947 when the visionary leaders of that time envisioned a prosperous and a successful country. But today Pakistan is in a great turmoil and is suffering from a stranglehold of economic, political and social crisis. Nevertheless, the situation of human rights in Pakistan is such that it has always been criticised and has put a bad name to the country. The people of this country have been deprived of their basic rights. The democracy could never flourish and has been ruthlessly crushed by Military rules many a times. Apart from that, many other socio-political elements like poverty, illiteracy, lack of good governance, corruption and lack of awareness contribute handsomely towards the declining human rights situation in Pakistan. All these factors unite and play their role leading us in to violations of the rights of people. Yet we have not learnt to unite under one flag as a singular Pakistani nation but are living as a crowd under the delusions of religious, cultural, political and social differences and are fanning the state towards absolute deterioration.

Better health facilities, enhanced educational standards and their provision thereof; shelter, clean drinking water, sanitation facilities and, above all, peace, stability and security of individuals are the fundamental rights of the people, which the state is responsible to provide and ensure in a sustainable and durable manner; yet the ground realities remain in contrast. One finds oneself between the devil and the deep blue sea, standing naked before the mirror, as there is no democratic and political culture that prevails here today. Democracy aside, we have not even enabled ourselves to a state where a nation respects its constitution as a cornerstone. We have been not only violating the constitution but have also been amending it to serve our ends. The most unprotected and insecure document in our country is our constitution, a document that guarantees the rights of individuals but its own rights are not guaranteed and that is the foremost root cause of all the violations in this land.

The mechanism on the whole is corrupt with a poor legal system. There are no public bodies to strengthen the system and the role of the civil society organisations remains limited. The organs of the state have a poor efficiency and there is no concept of equality before the law. Every man and woman is equal before the law but in Pakistan unfortunately there is a disparity in this internationally recognised and practiced maxim due to a certain influential few. We have legislated rules and regulations for everything but our major dilemma lies not in legislation but in the implementation of legislation. One of the main areas that is being ignored and not taken in to consideration is patriotism, nationalism and duty towards the beloved motherland. Where do we stand as a nation and where do we want to go is the real question that needs a real direction. Let us not let our grandchildren question us as to what the ideology of Pakistan was but rather let's endure and build upon it; while we still can. This is the first step towards a nation's unity. We do not only need unity but on the whole we, as Pakistanis, need reunification and rejuvenation.

In the end, it all comes down to education and awareness. This is not a storm in a tea cup but we need to elevate our standards of education and the provision of education to the masses. Today we remain caught up with issues like domestic violence against women, child labour, bonded labour, feudalism, Martial laws, infant mortalities, economic problems and many other social and political evils. We need to think and act with grave seriousness towards education and awareness-raising in order to come out of this moral vacuum that we, as a nation, have become. People have sacrificed their lives for this land. Let us not let their struggle and sacrifices die due to our misconduct, irresponsible attitude and an insane lack of interest towards Pakistan's social sector reforms. We will have to unite to save our country and to uphold human rights for without the respect, protection and fulfilment of human rights, no social change for betterment may ever be realised. It is very surprising to note, that people sometimes consider the civil society to reform the social sector and develop it all alone. This is not true for a change in a social set-up is brought about by the society itself. It is always the aggregate sum of the small contributions of the people that change the fate of nations. Birds of a feather must flock together and hence we all need to unite and work hard for the betterment of our country together and that we can only do so by upholding the spirit of human rights through awareness raising and education. If else wise, it may mean the end of civilization as we know it.

I merely wish to humbly surrender to you that no matter what country or continent we come from we are all basically the same human beings. We have the common human needs and concerns. We all seek happiness and try to avoid suffering regardless of our race, religion, nationality or political status. Human beings have the right to pursue happiness and live in peace and in freedom. As free human beings we can use our unique intelligence to try to understand ourselves and our world. But if we are prevented from using our creative potential, we are deprived of one of the basic characteristics of a human being. It is very often the most gifted, dedicated and creative members of our society who become victims of human rights abuses. Thus the political, social, cultural and economic developments of a society are obstructed by the violations of human rights. Therefore, the protection of these rights and freedoms are of immense importance both for the individuals affected and for the development of the society as a whole.

I, for one, am of a staunch conviction that individuals can make a difference in society. Every individual has a responsibility to help others move in the right direction and we must each assume that responsibility. A Buddhist monk, once said "To encourage myself in this altruistic attitude, I sometimes find it helpful to imagine myself standing as a single individual on one side, facing a huge gathering of all other human beings on the other side. Then I ask myself, 'Whose interests are more important?' To me it is quite clear that however important I may feel I am, I am just one individual while others are infinite in number and importance."

What my experiences have taught me so far is that our salvation lies in the essence and spirit of the respect for the rights of people. In the most immaculate, comprehensive and conclusive words, all I can submit is "Let us pledge to be pious and righteous in our deeds by sharing love, mercy and goodness with other people of the community in order to achieve the noblest state in the eyes of God. This indeed is what God Almighty demands of us and is the very essence and the rationale for granting this beautiful life to us."

The Defenceless Defenders

Someone once rightly said, "Security is just like oxygen. You cannot see it but you know it's there." Sense of security comes before security itself. If there is a sense of security one feels at ease and daily life can go on undisturbed without the need of extraordinary measures in attempting to make environment sound secure. On the contrary, at times, certain circumstances render the sense of security deplorable and there is felt the dire need of putting forth adequate security measures and mechanisms to secure the lives of the masses. Pakistan is engaged in, or shall we say, caught up in the midst of fighting terrorism where the terrorists are knocking at every door in the country to fight back in their own manner, which is no different from a guerrilla warfare tactic. This makes the situation volatile and asks every sane man and woman to act proactively towards assisting the authorities in putting an end to the menace. But are the said authorities also of the same mind is what makes one wonder all the time; keeping in view the intensity of what is going on and the ruthless level of lame response the government is coming back with.

I tend to lose my marbles in my effort to digest that we are fighting with terrorism at our frontiers in Waziristan but do not have adequate security measures in place inside our home. We never follow the principle of keeping the enemy at bay neither do we understand the policy of pre-empting a situation. All this adds up to the misery coupled by not having internal security mechanisms and procedures. We only deal with a situation once it rises up to a maximum threshold and slips out of hands. We have become reactive and I do not know when we would become proactive as a nation. Talking about ourselves as a nation I find it notable and worth stating that we are not exactly a nation but a mere crowd forced to live together. Nations have some character that is demonstrated in their lives but we, as Pakistanis, are simply showing the symbols of a crowd of people and nothing else. Be it the government, which is easy to blame, be it the law enforcement agencies or masses from any walk of life; all we can do is to level allegations and point fingers. But does this evade us of our civic sense? Could it sufficiently allow us to escape from our sense of belongingness and responsibility thereof? No, it would not. Hence we need to be ready and willing to make sacrifices and bring about positive development and not only surviving merely for a few dollars more. The word Pakistani does not denote a nation anymore; it just signifies a long lost nationality. I would like to say that it is time to reflect, it is a time for healing and not intolerance, and it is indeed the greatest test of a revolutionary transformation that we need to pass in order to prove that we still have the enzymes of a nation alive in us.

During the last couple of months the terrorism incidences have risen and the situation is getting worse. As we very well understand the need for gearing up ourselves and getting ready to fight back because it is a known psychological human behaviour that people first tend to be afraid of a situation but if it increases and occurs with more intensity and frequency; people find the courage to fight back and this is about time that Pakistan needs to unite and fight back this evil to the extent that this menace is thrown out of our beloved motherland. But what is the response of our authorities? What is it that the Interior Ministry and law enforcement is doing to protect the innocent masses of Pakistan? Increased number of policemen? Increased patrolling? Increased number of pickets and security check points? Is that the answer to all of this? No, but it perhaps lies somewhere else. It lies, so to speak, in the proactive approach of the government as well as having a proper sense of ownership coupled by long term and medium term strategic planning, without which all of us will merely remain aloof. Only a few days back there were attacks on FIA, police training academies, the GHQ and in Islamabad followed by attacks in Attok. The answer to all of this was planning a crackdown on suspects, increased security check points and more policemen to patrol etc. I wouldn't dare say it is wrong but indeed this is not enough or perfectly adequate.

Nonetheless, my professional endeavours exposed me to opportunities to deliver training sessions to the police department all across the Punjab and Islamabad. The impressions that I got from my experiences are rather depressing. I was once delivering a session at the police training academy, Sihala Islamabad. Whilst talking over tea to a few DSPs I intentionally deviated the focus of our discussion from our core point of refugee law to the existing police set up and the style and level of policing in Pakistan. I said to them that we are living in contemporary world of 2007 and yet our police department has not learnt the basic scientific skills in interrogation and investigation, forensic science and other scientific disciplines that the west has already mastered. Why is it that we cannot break the shell and do something appropriate in making our police, like our army, one of the best and highly competitive in the world? To that they unanimously replied that the problem lies in higher level bureaucracy of law enforcement, their unwillingness to bring about a positive change in the system, their inability to breathe the breaths of political wisdom and will needed to bring about such a change and the element of corruption existing therein.

I continue to wonder as to when would be the time when we would stop bowing to the false gods of money and material thereby working with a conviction towards the abolition of corruption from our society. For as long as that isn't rooted out law would continue to serve the needs of the influential few. Inasmuch as the police story goes; salaries of the lower staff are not raised according to the standard level, which adds to their already deteriorating miserable state and hence forces them to use other means to fulfil their financial needs. Lack of training and proper allotment of funds for equipment and arms only adds to their lack of service delivery and they hence do not, and for that matter, cannot render results with a strategic approach. They will keep on running after issues as and when those occur. I say it is about time that we should all stop thinking about ourselves only and begin to ponder over our future generations for once. After all, our children and youth are not safe from terrorism any longer and its affects and recent events have proved the point very well indeed. It is my child today and it could be yours tomorrow; lest we refuse to understand. Where do we stand in this war against the militants when those who are to guard us remain unguarded themselves?

I, for one, pity our young police officers and am one of those who, rather than pointing fingers towards them and singling them out, comprehend for a fact that they will remain undefended and helpless unless and until we train and groom them on latest techniques in policing and security measures coupled by allotting sufficient funds to them so that they could remain not only trained but also fully equipped to face the challenges that they are exposed to in these difficult times. If we look at the police pickets all across our towns we can easily see that these police officers do not even have protective helmets, flak jackets or at least proper arms. How can we expect them to defend and protect us given that they feel unprotected themselves is the question of the day. Their lower salaries and benefits is another area to tackle with. Under such low wages and remuneration, their morale remains low and self-esteem buried somewhere next to their traumatised subconscious. The government needs to come up with a grand design including some sweepstakes in order to equip these poor policemen with adequate and appropriate arsenal required to combat terrorism at home. The army is doing her bit at the borders but securing our home remains the vital responsibility of the Ministry of Interior and law enforcement agencies. Many policemen have lost their lives in their effort against terrorism yet nothing seems to have changed and will not change because we only believe in increasing the number of defenceless pickets everywhere. Our people will not be protected until our defenders- our defenceless defenders, are fully equipped with state-of-the-art technology that they require.

The Coming of Noah (PBUH)

The recent floods in Pakistan have caused devastation at a scale greater than and beyond Pakistan's approach. The government has clearly mentioned this many a times till now thereby admitting the fact that the devastation has gone beyond their control. In a series of spells of heavy and continuous rainfall the waters in all rivers have swollen causing their banks to erupt and allowing the waters to roam around wildly across the country's towns and villages destroying whatever comes in their way. The flooding started from the Kabul River and engulfed other rivers and water systems causing destruction of unmatched precedence. Taking 1500 lives already and affecting 3 million people directly or indirectly, as I write this, is just being termed as the beginning. The monsoon systems are further developing and there is an expectation that there will be an upsurge during the weeks to come. This is a calamity which, according to the UN Secretary General, has not been witnessed before and surpassing the scales of the October 8 earthquake, the Haiti earthquake as well as other flooding situations.

While the government has started pleading before the international community to raise funds and help Pakistan in this time of great human emergency, the UN estimates the need to be 460 million dollars for quick relief and billions of dollars later on in terms of reconstruction and rehabilitation. "This disaster is far from over" said Ban-Ki Moon tonight while addressing a joint conference with President Zardari. Our President has finally got some time off his busy schedule of visiting other countries to have a look in to his for a change. This reminds me of how we criticize the government, President Zardari and his administration for not doing anything for the country but to me the cause and effect analysis has to be put in a different direction. It is directly narrated by the God himself in the Quran that the heads of state imposed on a people will not be different from the people that they represent. If analysed, this means that the government is an exact reflection of who we are and hence pointing our fingers towards them means pointing the fingers towards ourselves. The people from the government are people from amongst ourselves; then why the outcry? If we start to take this religious principle in to consideration with faith it tells us that in order to correct a state and her government the people of that state will have to correct themselves and hence the path to resolution is very simple; lest we wouldn't understand.

The problem is that our priorities are reversed and we need to put them in order so that we can find salvation and can properly address our problems. However, we are not able to keep a perfect or at least some balance between spirituality and worldly logic. Whenever in trouble, we try to reach out the worldly medicine first and then when everything else fails we turn to God in the end, which I believe is not worthy of us given that we all have faith in the fact that it is God who is the master of our lives and this world. Therefore, we need to set our priorities and always refer to the God in the first place and then other prescriptions afterwards. Whenever we have a headache we always resort to Aspirin but never do consider that, according to the Quran, it is God who sends all the sickness upon us and it is God who sends their cure. Keeping our right hand on the head firmly and reciting the first chapter of the Quran "Fatiha" three times is the basic cure for headaches but we do not know this and do not in a way have a strong and staunch conviction in this medicine. By the way, I have tried it many a times and it really cures with magical impact. Now this may seem more of a ritual to many people but scientifically it has been proven that most headaches are due to air-locking in the head and holding the head firmly for some time releases that and cures the headache. However, we need to have faith in such things as Muslims in order to enable such things to work for us.

Nevertheless, the story of Noah's flood (and Noah's ark) is so famous a story that has been revealed unto the mankind in the Holy Bible, the Holy Quran and other scriptures and it is widely told and narrated in different cultures and parts of the world that almost every one living in all the continents are familiar with it. What is in that story that makes it so famous across the globe has the answer to many questions. In this story, it is revealed that God got so angry with the people for not following the true discipline that he instructed Noah PBUH to construct an ark and save those who were truthful and pious and wiped off the rest in the great flood and begin anew. Noah PBUH kept warning people of the flooding situation but the deaf wouldn't listen and the blind wouldn't see. This whole tale is repeatedly told and understood, as it emerges both in the Bible and the Quran, but the peoples of today are different from those people who couldn't listen or see. Yet there is a difference for the contemporary world of today i.e. there is no more the coming of the Noah PBUH and we have to learn from this tale for ourselves and our future generations.

The rationale, for getting this discussion in to a religious perspective was to find out the exact reasons of the cause of floods. While many people would blame climatic change and global warming etc. it is to contest the reasons told to us by God, so that we could get our priorities straightened, as discussed above. The reasons of such calamities and natural disasters are proven to be related to people getting swayed away from the word of God, from piousness and righteousness, from the message of one God and attempting to lead life in the way and manner prescribed by God Himself and His messengers. It is said that there are two different kinds of catastrophes, the natural catastrophe (external) and the moral catastrophe (internal). We can safely argue that the greater the internal catastrophe the greater will be the external catastrophe. Therefore, in order to find a solution we need to look at ourselves and improve ourselves by improving our moral disasters in order to reduce the natural disasters.

This flood will pass by yet there could be more in different forms and to fight against them we need to fight within ourselves by challenging our 'self' so that we can raise it to a level that can divert the external disasters for the times to come. To test this, just look at the places where such disasters take place and look at the moral levels of the people living in those places and then compare that to the areas which are considerably safe and their people are rather better off in terms of moral values. May Allah SWT keep us safe from all such natural disasters and allow us the strength to fight with ourselves and raise our spirits and moralities. However, such calamities should not only be looked upon as a punishment from God but also as a great test and reminder of God; for those who understand, for those who can listen and see, for those who are wise and for those who have faith-verily these are the signs of God if we understand. May Allah SWT bestow His truest blessings on us all… Ameen!

Peshawar; a centre of lost civilizations

The concept of change in the world is rather permanent. This can be easily understood by looking at the map of the countries and cities. In ancient times, with different invaders and conquerors, the maps kept on changing permanently from one time span to another. However, the nations and peoples that have survived change are only those who have learnt to change themselves with the change in their respective circumstances. Yet there have been many who have and still continue to resist change but their efforts are insignificant. The reason is that change has to come given that we live in a world of evolution and such a world is prone to changes all the times known to mankind. The great city, or valley, of Peshawar is the kind of a place that has remained a centre of attraction to various civilizations over time. A city that was founded some 2,000 years ago holds in her arms a treasure of civilizations, traditions and cultures. Peshawar is the oldest living city in Asia. Peshawar has played an important role throughout recorded history being the most ancient city amongst central, south and west Asia. It is due to this very geographic significance that Peshawar has long served as a trade centre for Afghanistan, Central Asia and the Middle East. The one who controls Peshawar controls this important junction.

It was the Kushans of the Tucharian origin from far-east China who founded the city 2,000 years ago. The great Kushan king moved the capital from Pushkalavati (Charsadda), which was kept as capital by the Gandhara civilization; to Purushpura (city of men) now called Peshawar. Before that time it was the eastern capital of the Gandhara civilization under the ancient Indo-Iranian kingdom. Afterwards, the city fell to Alexander due to which the influx of Indo-Greeks became greater in the city. It was also in this era that Buddhism was introduced in the valley and remained the largest religion till the coming of Islam. Hence Peshawar became one of the greatest centres for Buddhist learning and civilization. Further on, Peshawar was taken over by the Turks and taken on by the Mughals in the 16th century. It was at this time that Akbar the grandson of the first Mughal king Babur named this Purushpura valley as Peshawar, which means "The place at the Frontier" in Persian. The Mughals turned this city in to the "city of flowers" by extensive plantation. The city was dominated by the

Pashtuns from the Sulaiman Mountains of Southern Afghanistan. The Pashtuns had accepted Islam after annexation of Southern Afghanistan by the Arab Empire from Khurassan. Afterwards, during the reign of Sher Shah Suri the Grand Trunk Road (GT Road) was built and there came a boom in trade and transit in this valley. With the British colonial designs the Mughal dynasty could not survive and along came the British to rule here and left after the partition when Peshawar was annexed to Pakistan in 1947. Historically, Peshawar has remained a home to many great Muslim scholars, writers, poets, Sufis, bureaucrats, technocrats, scientists, traders and soldiers etc. This city has accepted and shaped herself due to the different civilizations that have lived here from one time in history to another.

In the contemporary Pakistan it is the city of smoke and pollution and in a few years those who can find a single flower in the once city of flowers would be rewarded for their sighting abilities. The city is now a host to dust, pollution and noise. The civilizations have lost their traces and marks in this valley however now the only discussion here is about the prevailing corrupt politics, terrorism, economic problems, social issues and religious degenerations. In the last 60 years or so, after the independence of Pakistan, our leadership has gifted this rich land of civilizations and cultures that always lived together in harmony; with chaos and conflicts; with problems and issues. Needless to say, it seems as if we are not able to understand how to live in harmony and how to take care of our problems and take them towards solutions. People have always been misled by the politicians at one hand whereas by the so called religious clerics on the other. This city today is the centre of all the economic, social, religious, cultural and political problems ever known to mankind.

The education system is in a mess and the level of illiteracy is high alongside poverty and lack of income earning opportunities. This is of course coupled by lack of awareness in the masses of the city about their rights and about their own good and betterment. This causes abuse of power and exploitation of the poor. During the last decade, under the Gen. Musharraf kingdom and afterwards under the MMA rule and now including the ANP, one thing that has suffered a lot is the infrastructure. With suicide attacks and bombs exploding all across; the infrastructure has been affected. Environmental degradation is only to name another Pandora's Box. The city of flowers knows nothing today that can be termed green. The thought that Peshawar is geographically a valley does not even comes to the mind of the ordinary nowadays due to its existing state. There are no parks for families to recreate and for kids and children to grow healthy. The ones that are there are in such a state that people do not want to visit them. Mentioning of the dust, noise, overcrowding, road conditions, traffic jams and transportation services makes the indigenous peoples perplexed up to an extent of virtual suffocation. If one picks up an economics textbook, one will find all economic problems mentioned there; existing in the city. This indeed is a shame to note that once the Rhinos inhabited this valley. Whereas today one can't find anything green and hence the animal and plant kingdoms have said goodbye to a place that was once their favourite abode. This valley is now a jungle inhabited by social animals. This is again strange that rather than doing something about correcting the problems the Peshawarites are struggling to learn how to live and survive in the midst of such problems, which to most is the easy way out, which it isn't.

What happened in this city is remarkable to note since due to lack of wisdom and will of the influential to bring about a positive change Peshawar is what she is today. Therefore, it can be said safely that nothing can bring about a positive, visible and constructive change in this city unless the people unite in this cause and embark on something that can be termed as a GRAND DESIGN that needs to be implemented here for betterment of the people. Such a grand design should include awareness, education, health, environment, economy, peace, justice and governance as its main components.

Nevertheless, there is another turn around that is required. People have waited and looked upon their leadership to change everything for good over the last sixty years or so and this is what they have gifted us. Therefore, the need of the day is to think otherwise and start chipping in our bits in order to change everything that surrounds the city. The change has to come in a bottoms-up approach now. We can no longer continue standing at the bottom and looking at the top. The people of Peshawar need to take the first step, to think positively, to take charge and rebuild their city and their lives all over again to a level where once again Peshawar be called the city of flowers, the centre of civilizations and cultures and a place at the Frontier where craftsmen and the intellectuals, the rich and the poor and the skilful and the tradesman live together in peace and harmony with each other. This will only be achieved if the aforementioned grand design is implemented by the people and not by the government because they wouldn't; besides they would've if they wanted to. And for that, I reckon, the first step would be to start raising awareness of the masses and such aware masses would automatically force their leadership to do what is required. As they say, political change is brought about by the people and not by the leaders; hence that will have to be the case here otherwise it may even be the end of civilization in Peshawar. Given the fact that Peshawar is the Asian goldmine for its geographic significance, once uplifted through the grand design, this city will once again become the centre of culture and civilization. Peshawar controls the transit for South Asia, Central Asia and the Middle East and only this very factor can change the lives of the people; provided that this city is developed and not only the city but the people too who have, after many years of hopelessness, lost all their hopes and hence remain bewildered in the centre of lost civilizations.

In Search of Pakistan

It is widely understood and believed that nations are recognised by some virtues. This means that there are some virtues that are demonstrated by different nations differently and hence those determine their characteristics in a unique manner thereby differentiating them from other nations. Of these virtues, the most significant are surely the value systems, cultures, customs and traditions. All these factors work in combination with each other in shaping and fostering groups, communities, societies and largely nations. This is what enables nations in differentiating themselves from other nations in giving colour to this world. This also is a factor that determines, in a country, whether the people together are a bunch of people only, living as chaotic crowds, or whether they are living in harmony with each other as a nation. Now if we are to be convicted of this very discussion, it would mean that the same contributing factors discussed above also shape the fates of nations, as nations, given that the strengths and weaknesses of the nations depend on these elements. Similarly, it would also mean that the nations that are strong, have powerful and binding value systems, cultures, traditions and customs etc. and the nations that are rather feeble have weak value systems and cultures etc. Therefore, one has to understand the exact force of power these elements have in shaping the past, present and future of a nation.

Pakistan got independence in 1947 and has evolved, so to speak, as a country during the past six decades. This is a country that has got its liberation from the imperial British rule with a huge struggle of different people and a massive fight against such tyranny. During this was the factor that made all the people belonging to Pakistan come closer to each other in demanding a separate state for them. In this regard, the contributing factors were again the same, that is to say, the people came closer and united because they were the same indigenous people having similar customs, traditions, culture and value systems. Had these factors not been present Pakistan might never have been created. In this notion, it is also to be understood, that this was the root cause giving rise to the two-nation theory, envisioned by the Pakistani leadership that was later to become the ideology of Pakistan. Hence such people of the Indo-Pak united for a cause and got themselves a separate and free independent homeland. People started living together in the country and the factors that helped them were the same; they were the same peoples having similar backgrounds. However, as the time passed by this land has seen and has witnessed occasions and incidences of disunity that are beyond imagination. What is the driving force behind those disuniting acts is not that hard to understand; it is the fact that people of this land have lost conviction and faith in their own cultures and traditions that once united them to create the country. *Drifting away from one's culture leaves one stranded in the middle of nowhere till the time his suffocation strangles him.* Those who drift away from their culture are actually moving away from themselves; and then there starts a process so dangerous in nature that it may know no boundary and hence has the audacity to bring a stop to a nation on the whole. History is evident of the fact that the nations who have forgotten their cultures have been wiped off the planet; which is exactly what is also preached by wise men like Rumi.

If we examine Pakistan as a case point, it is not hard to find out that the people of Pakistan have embarked on this journey happily intending to forget their culture and norms and becoming prey to the odds in the society. Pakistan was never known as a place where terrorism lurks, where there are suicide bombers, where there is extremism and absolute intolerance, where people take the law in their own hands, where the race for material is the first priority in the hustle bustle of life. Today if I look at my motherland, for which, once people fought with their lives; looks on to be a place wherein different people of different casts, origins, cultures, traditions, religious sects, races and regions are living or are rather forced to live together given the intolerance in the society. I can easily spot a Balouch, a Pathan, a Sindhi, a Punjabi, a Sunni, a Barelvi, a Shia and many others but even after trying hard I cannot, repeat cannot, identify a Pakistani. This was never our country. I can also understand that these differences were always there but were hidden somewhere under the fabric of Pakistan's national dress, yet people have happily taken off that dress and are now singing and dancing naked without it.

Pakistan was once a land of harmony and peace, of tranquillity and patience, of cultural richness and traditional hospitality, of respect and dignity for all. What happened to that land, what happened to that country? Well this can be comprehended only with the argument that people have lost their direction and their identity. People have lost their culture and customs. Today, in the contemporary Pakistan, her citizens feel ashamed to speak in the national language, feel backward for wearing the national dress, feel bad about belonging to this country and feel rather awkward in the exercise of the culture and traditions. This is so due to the fact that people have stopped taking pride in their country and the traditions and culture for which once this land was blessed as a progressive Asian country. This is a country which has had numerous artists, literary personalities, political figures of great stature and ever loving and humble people. This is a country where once patience and sacrifice were every man's traits. The culture of Pakistan is a culture of peace and love and of Muslim unity and resilience. For decades all the people having religious, regional and racial differences have lived in peace and harmony with each other. However, forgetting the culture has ousted us of a once civilized society. Although there is no harm in learning from other cultures and doing things with innovation and thinking outside the box but then that has to be coupled by a state where people do not think bad about who they really are. Modernism is always a good sign however the way modernism is defined is really important. People here are in fact getting westernised under the delusions of getting modernised. Modernisation is not Westernisation. We can be absolutely modern in a very traditional manner and we do not really have to use slang in order to provide proof of modernism. We do not similarly have to drift away from our culture and adopt a western culture so that the people of the world can call us modern. And if this were so, then it means that we are indirectly calling nations like the Iranians and the Chinese, not really modern.

Hence what we need to do is to recapture and revitalise the Pakistani identity and the true Pakistani value so as to enable ourselves once again to be proclaimed a nation and not merely a crowd. This can only be done by promoting our culture, our traditions, our language and other social, religious and political norms and values that make us reflect Pakistanism. The land is thirsty for this to revive and take the lead role in our daily lives, if we are to survive this hectic and chaotic environment under which we are forced to live these days. Pakistan's culture is that of harmony, peace, love and respect. Pakistan's culture is that of family unity and living with a grace. Unless and until this pro-cultural patriotism inflicted modernism is induced, we cannot dream of a better Pakistan. Hence there is a dire need for waking up from this material dream and looking deeper in to the realities of fostering, once again, a Pakistan that was once known for its socio-political and religious and cultural harmony. This can only be done by understanding that we are not those who bomb but who bloom and let blossom, who are law abiding, who have adequate religious and cultural harmony. Let us not allow this regional and cultural diversity destroy us but let us celebrate it to our greater advantage by developing and building upon our strengths whilst we still can. That will only be done if we revitalise our culture by taking pride in it. Let us try and reform this society by promoting love against anger and hate and by transforming the cultural and regional differences in to an understanding and tolerance for cultural and regional diversity.

I am convicted that I am a true Pakistani. I am modern in my unique manner. I can rise to the top due to my culture and traditions in this insane world of cut-throat competition and material. Urdu is my language, Shalwar Qamees is my dress, rich folk music is my tune, cultural diversity is my identity, respect and dignity is what my ancestors have taught me, love and peace is my inborn trait, tolerance and patience is my second nature; and "Pakistani" is my name.

Blessed be thy name; Pakistan…!

Happy Independence Day?

The Independence Day of Pakistan is 14th August. This very day symbolises the struggle of our forefathers in demanding and afterwards successfully obtaining a separate state for their future generations; for us however, the significance of the day is seen every year through different events organised throughout the country in order to show solidarity with the homeland. Many colourful events are planned and executed in sharing a unified mutual attitude towards the term 'independence' yet to many the interpretations are diversified and varied. While many would contest my view that the independence of Pakistan had to do more with alteration of the world map and less with bringing about a physiological and psychological change in the lives of the indigenous people. Yet the amazing fact that was seen in the shape of Pakistan was made to be there forever.

What exactly is independence to us? Is it merely a sense of having a state where one can roam around easily or does this has to do something with values as well? Soon after the creation of the motherland there started political disputes and power struggle and with that happening is it safe to call such an independence an independence is what one's mind always wonders. The political leadership, since then, has been busy in their power struggle and in that race they have left far behind all the known norms and values on which this country was formed. This race has proven to be the best tool favouring corruption at all levels that just goes on unchecked and at a pace never known before to mankind.

Independence today is nothing more than celebrating just a single day reminding us of all the struggles that led to the creation of this country on the face of this planet, but that ends on the very same day without having to do anything in the lives of the people. Civilised nations understand very well in the words of Thomas Jefferson that independence and ignorance cannot move together. However, when we look at the education level and standards in Pakistan, we can easily analyse what independence we are talking about. Living under the clutches of foreign aid and the IMF we cannot really pronounce ourselves independent; or can we? The majority of the nation has been left uneducated to fuel the feudal only and that has resulted today in a nation that has no direction at all and that believes it has got nothing to do in the development of the country.

Mohammad Ali Jinnah wanted us to learn Unity, Faith and Discipline. These were the main message he always gave to the nation in order to make us grow as a nation however the level of our unity today can be easily judged by seeing that we are living under the delusion of being Punjabis, Pathans, Sindis and Balochis where finding a man called Pakistani is almost impossible. The same is the case with our faith, which is acting like a beheaded animal being ruled under the poison of religious differences, which is beyond comprehension given that the God, the Prophet and the Book are only one and not many. As for the last message of the Quaid, discipline, I wouldn't even make a comment because its current level can be easily seen all around us.

The respect for elders is a long gone case, our cultural values are deteriorating, we are happily becoming a moral vacuum and yet we would not understand that independence was not meant only to rid ourselves of the British rule but it was supposed to be enshrined in our daily lives, as Islam teaches us in general, as the Quaid meant in particular and as Iqbal envisioned throughout his life. It is the independence of the soul and mind from the ever so attractive ills of the west to which this society has become a welcoming host. The west took all the good of the eastern societies and there is nothing wrong in it however we are taking all the ills or bad of the west and there is nothing right in it. We believe we are being modernised under the illusion of getting westernised, which we wouldn't, as we couldn't and in a real sense we shouldn't.

What is required today is that sense of belonging and unity without which we will never be able to enjoy our independence on the 14th August every year with a feeling of satisfaction. We have started taking pride in fake gods and are hence moving away from our cultural and religious values. What we need to focus on is paving the way for a better Pakistan by uniting under one flag and feeling the pain of others. The recent floods have also failed to unite us under one flag and that is a very jeopardising signal. We will have to open the eyes of our heart and then try to see Pakistan. Listening to a national song in my car today made me break down in tears. It was the famous "Watan ki Mitti

Gawah rehna" sung by Nayyar-a-Noor because when I heard her saying "Watan ki mitti azeem hai tu… Azeem tar hum bana rahe hain" it made me think of how we are busy in making our Pakistan "Azeem tar" and on this note I leave the readers think and decide themselves keeping faith in what the Quaid said, "Do your duty and have faith in God, there is no power on earth that can undo Pakistan; it has come to stay."

And there goes the PPP manifesto "Roti, Kapra aur Makan"

It was a little after 'Aftar' tonight that I was watching TV when my wife made me tune in to BBC's programme "Have Your Say" being broadcasted live and the issue under discussion was the floods in Pakistan and the existing trust deficit. Whilst watching the programme I felt like thanking my wife for making me watch this and cursing myself for following her recommendation simultaneously. However, as they say, truth, no matter how bitter, prevails. I saw that programme followed by a story on CNN, which threw more light in that direction. Having being richly enlightened for that particular half an hour gave me an inspiration and made me wonder that at times great disasters occur in order to reveal upon us as to how insanely dull and dead we have become, as those natural disasters shake us to consider such things that we take for granted. The outcry relating to the corruption of the Pakistani government was always there yet we put no heed to how badly that could and does affect us. While most of the country is affected by the floods I term the whole of the country affected by this menace called Corruption.

The BBC programme "Have Your Say" tonight was focusing on the reluctance of the international community in providing aid to the flood affected Pakistan due to the trust deficit that exists because of the corruption in the Pakistani government, and that I find to be true. Even though funds are being transferred to Pakistan and, as a colleague tells me, about half a billion dollars has reached home and more will come yet my distress is not exactly about the fact that whether the funds are flowing or not. My anguish has to do mostly with how the world is looking at Pakistan and since this government is elected democratically, the corruption is being affixed to the nation and not only the government anymore, which I believe is a devastating sign bound to bring bad name to the nation on the whole. An African commentator said it is perhaps because of Islam-o-phobia that the US and other western nations are not showing signs of solidarity; however, that idea was soon ridiculed since it was a ridicules cynicism of course. Humanitarian aid I reckon has got nothing to do with race, religion and creed etc. since it was given to Indonesia and other Islamic countries including Pakistan in the past. However, aid has to do a lot with the credibility of the government to which it is entrusted. And in this regard, the Pakistan of today needs no words of explanation. The final statement made by Imran Khan, Leader of PTI, had great significance; as he stated that the President is busy asking money from the world whereas he should be focusing on generating money and grouping people from within and at home. This factor is missing and has to be mounted higher than ever before, so is the need.

The CNN on the other hand focused on the Kerry-Zardari joint press conference wherein a question was asked from the president that since the funds are not coming in and it is being related to the reputation of the president himself for being a corrupt man, to which he had no straight answer and hence had to stall the question. All this is happening at the same time the British press is advising their PM to "count his fingers after shaking hands with Pakistan's Mr ten per cent" only adds to the misery. I believe it is not about foreign aid coming in or not but it is about raising voice against the malice of corruption that has now openly started to eat up all the resources, reputation and traditions of the country. This is indeed a testing time but it will pass by the grace of God and we will surely emerge as a nation that stands by to such testing times but my worry will never fade away given that the rich enlightenment that I received tonight will haunt me for months and even years. Having been brought up to see this day where my country is getting all the blame for issues like corruption cuts me in to pieces. Is this the democracy we fought for? Is this the government we elected by voting in their favour? It is indeed correct to mention that today it is the Peoples Party's government but in this government the Peoples Party of the legendary and one of the greatest visionaries and leaders Mr Zulfiqar Bhutto is nowhere to be seen. Peoples Party have always had a slogan, a visionary manifesto "Roti, Kapra aur Makan" mainly because it was the party of the labourers it was the party of the poor. However, today our nation is deprived of all these three elements under their rule. This is indeed as embarrassing as it is unfortunate that these basic necessities of life are what the common man of our country is in search for today in a world where such things are considered a pre-requisite to livelihood. All this happens at a time when our so called leaders have alienated us, even under such troublesome times when the common man looks at the government to be his saviour. This has to end before this becomes The End.

Infringing the right to life

I am instigated by a report presented in the parliament recently to write on indeed a very shocking and utterly depressing issue. The Federal Minister for Human Rights Mr Mumtaz Alam Gilani has informed the National Assembly about more than 180 suicides in Pakistan only in one year. Pakistan used to be a country where incidents like suicides used to be major news and today suicide is not news really but its increasing number is. What is it that made this society move in that direction? It is obviously something, as Mr Gilani pointed out, related to issues like poverty, inflation and unemployment. It is also very easy for the Speaker National Assembly to conclude the issue by stating that it is the responsibility of parliamentarians, civil society and media to discourage such a trend. But it is not absolutely just to merely consider the job done through these few intangible steps in trying to help the society in putting an end to this devastating trend that seems to be emerging rapidly now. There is yet more that needs to be done in this regard.

What makes one wonder is nothing other than the fact that problems like the price hike; economic downturn, lawlessness; injustice and joblessness etc. have actually always been there in our country. We have been struggling in our 63 years history against similar problems, yet there has never been such a high figure in terms of suicides. I believe this issue is of grave seriousness and requires immediate attention. This immediate attention is not to say that economic problems are the reason for such incidences and there is a need to discourage this trend. On the contrary, one needs to, above all, appreciate and understand the root-cause of the problem. If poverty and economic downturn is the main reason for those 180 suicides in Pakistan, then corresponding figures must have also been there in the past 6 decades. However, this is not the case and hence one can conclude that perhaps there is some other reason attached to these suicides. The problems so highlighted are certainly the underlying reasons, and not the causes, of these suicides as one can comprehend that due to poverty, unemployment and inflation etc. there are people who were forced to put an end to their lives. I find myself convicted of the fact that the main root-cause of these suicides is just one element, which is hopelessness. The similar problems, as discussed above, were always there but people were not taking their lives because they could somehow see a ray of hope that would promise them a way out of such miseries. I gather that this is the time for the state to immediately wake up from the ever promising dream of a better Pakistan and take adequate steps in order to fulfil it, if there is any political wisdom and political will left, which has already become a rare commodity in Pakistan. People of this beautiful country are forced to commit suicides because they feel absolutely hopeless.

Taking one's life with one's own hands is not an easy thing and being Muslims we also understand very well that one who commits suicide surrenders one's hope for paradise. I can't honestly imagine the level of a person's hopelessness that inclines him to take a step, just to end his misery, in a way that refuses him his natural abode in the heaven. This, in reality, is the level of hopelessness that an average Pakistani is perhaps going through today. And this is the gravity of the problem in hand. We will never be able to put an end to this merely by organising seminars and walks and raising awareness of the people in discouraging this trend, but this adverse situation will only cease to exist when the root-cause is addressed, which is a man's hopelessness of a better life that renders upon him the minimum standards of living known to man. People today are in a state where their thoughts are challenged on a daily basis by witnessing the atrocities going on in a democratic nation and when they can't see an end to that or even a slight ray of hope; they decide to let go of everything that was once dear to them. Therefore, we require concentrated efforts to induce an environment in this country that encourages people to remain positive, at least, and for that people need to see concrete steps and policies in that direction and not merely words. The people of this nation are bored of hearing about better employment opportunities, controlled inflation as well as poverty alleviation. The time has come for one to work progressively for poverty alleviation and not for the elimination of the poor. We need to take this nation away from the clutches of the IMF by introducing development projects, creating jobs, reducing imports and increasing exports. We can still do it but only if we still have the dedication for Pakistan and not for ourselves. If the country is progressive, all her citizens enjoy such progress and in turn their lives are automatically improved but this requires pro-Pakistan policies in terms of education, health and agriculture sector reforms. With this, I am sure that not even a single citizen of our beloved country would even think of ending his life.

The most fundamental and basic human right enshrined in any given human rights instrument is the right to life. In this connection, it is encouraging to note that, the suicides report was highlighted by the Federal Minister for Human Rights, who is well known to me by virtue of my professional endeavours. The reason for stating this is that, in him, I see a light for bringing about constructive change in the society. He is not only a very senior member of the Pakistan Peoples' Party but is a true social worker as well. Since his inception, as the Minister, I have seen the Ministry intending to join hands with the civil society and encouraging a public-civil society partnership, which is the true requirement of the day since it opens avenues for the NGOs and the government to join hands and work together as a singular force against all odds in the society; the only way to make Pakistan again, a compassionate society. People have started to commit suicides because their rights are not fulfilled or given to them, which causes frustration and such quadrupled frustrations cause depression resulting ultimately in suicides. In order to resolve this state, of the people's minds, there is felt a strong need for the government to prove her commitment to the cause of making Pakistan a welfare state; a state that, in the words of Mr Aitezaz Ehsan, loves her citizens like a mother. Nonetheless, such commitment cannot come merely from speeches but actions, as they say actions speak louder than words. If we are committed to the cause of uprooting this evil, as per Ms Fehmida Mirza's statement, than we need to financially and technically equip the Human Rights ministry of Pakistan, whose funding at the moment is not enough at all. This shows the commitment of the government with regards to improving the overall human rights condition of the country. This becomes even more significant to be highlighted because today's Pakistan is a state that has recently completed the ratification of core human rights conventions and that the international bill of rights is now legally binding upon Pakistan. I find it rather depressing to imagine a country in which international bill of rights is legally binding and that very country's Human Rights Ministry is facing shortage of funding coupled by an increase in people taking their lives and depriving themselves of their most fundamental right to life.

One finds oneself between the devil and the deep blue sea in such circumstances but where there is a will there is a way. By vigorously strengthening the human rights ministry many issues would be addressed and many violations would be taken note of and hence there would become a redress forum available to people and their voices would be heard and their problems resolved. This would induce a kind of an environment where all such people deprived of their rights would have at least a hope for their rights to be taken care of and ultimately this will result in the betterment of their lives in terms of their rights, in a way that would reduce their frustration, depression and largely their hopelessness and hence an overall reduction in the suicide cases will be seen. It is also necessary to remember that all problems cannot be resolved by the government, and therefore a public, media and civil society partnership will remain as the master key to Pakistan's rights based issues and problems linked directly with the lives of the people. It is never too late to take the right decision in embarking on a journey in bringing about a major positive change. If right steps are taken in the right direction, many problems are addressed properly and amicable resolutions are reached. The issues, such as suicides, are related to the psychological mind-set of people and in order to change that; strong and concrete steps need to be taken that result in lessening of the violations of people's rights.

Of Love and Beauty: a Quest

We live in a world of mysteries and myths. A world that is full of surprises and unique events that shape the course of our lives in becoming what we are, at any point in time. Hence it would only be fitting to state that we are a being dependent and not fully free of circumstance and destiny for it is indeed what develops our being through time and we learn and mature with age. Therefore, it is not entirely incorrect to phrase that it is actually the experience that enables us in finding and pursuing the paths in our lives. However, experiences can be enriched by those who happen to have a good observation for it is the absolute observation that nurtures experience. Moreover, it is said that those who have a creative and imaginative mind can develop better observation. Therefore, to me, knowledge is the comprehensive embodiment of imagination that surfaces in observation and finally ripens through the reinforcement of experience thereby inculcating knowledge. This in fact is the short story of life.

When I was a young man, my father used to tell me that there are things that I would only understand with time. A concept I could not digest in those youthful days. I only wish now that if I could have, I might have been a wiser person today. However, this is how nature works and one cannot reverse the flow of stream in which our lives flow. He used to say that I would only be able to realize and appreciate the love for a child when I would have my own. Again, I quarrelled within myself and said no to that thinking that I know all there is to know about it already. Yet after having my own child I now do agree to whatever he said to the extent that I am convicted of the fact that my child would not be able to understand this very idea until he may have his own. The point I am trying to make here is that when my father told me such things I had imagination and could imagine what it means to know based on my observation however I was lacking the age, time and experience that enables one in appreciating what it takes to know. In conclusion, this is how knowledge is attained or it might perhaps not be incorrect to put that knowledge is not only about knowing what it means to be or to have but also about knowing what it really takes to be or to have.

Nonetheless, we, as humans, endeavour to identify and take on our own paths and directions in order to reach our destiny on the basis of knowledge that we acquire over time in helping us pave our journey, or better still, the voyage; called life. This indeed is the very essence of what brings colour in the fabric of our lives and therefore make this world beautiful. This world might not have been beautiful, had this colour not been an integral ingredient, in this very recipe called life. We find ourselves completely different from others but still we can relate to other people in one way or another. No matter how different, we still find our reflection in others. This is an absolute case of 'different means for a singular end.' We are connected one way or the other. We are dependent one way or the other.

Knowledge is hence not complete without experience, which is attained through age and hence life gives us knowledge and wisdom through an aging process only. And this process is uniquely a never-ending one, which is the reason why the wisest of men upon meeting their demise have concluded that they have known only so little. It is therefore time that intends to fathom knowledge, no matter how inaccurate no matter how incomplete, knowledge that is attained through imagination, observation and experience. What we consider to be correct today might not be correct tomorrow. This is because over time we mature and knowledge is enriched every passing day. This is the entire beauty of the world and as it is encompassed in a mere sentence by the beautiful words of the Prophet (SAWW) *'God is beautiful and He loves beauty'* for it is indeed so fitting a matter with life as well. But I wonder why did he say that? What does it really mean that God is beautiful? If He loves beauty then is it that He hates ugliness? Indeed that is the very idea since beauty being referred to here is not only physical or of matter alone. Beauty carries a wider philosophical meaning here. Beauty in this regard means of matter, spirituality as well as nature of things and beings. Therefore, this puts us on a challenge to make ourselves beautiful and to beautify things around us, and beautify ourselves in the process. Being or becoming beautiful does not refer to physical form alone but include and in fact in meaning surpasses the inner beauty of everything. Therefore, beautifying would mean promoting love against hatred, envy against jealousy, dignity against ego and honour against selfishness. This may seem a simple task yet it is not that straight forward. Our big egos, our inert esteem and our proclaimed self-righteousness urge us not to pave the way for beautifying ourselves and others around us. We fuel ourselves and our souls with materialistic merchandise and with selfish enzymes which is what stops us and makes us ugly and hence takes us farther away from beauty. Indeed we are our own greatest enemies.

Vanity, corruption, immorality, intolerance and jealousy are but only a few examples of what our egos can do to us and thence we become demons in flesh and bone. We start fighting amongst ourselves for superiority, showing each other anger and displaying hatred and jealousy and what not in this vicious struggle for survival without putting heed to the fact that we are but made to love each other, to cherish and comfort and help each other, to display mutual respect and to respect the mutual dignity of each other. Of all these evils, one greater than the other, vanity is but the ugliest for it is vanity indeed that ignites other evils and hence can be rightly termed as the mother of all evil or the devil itself. Self-praise is what we love the most whereas vanquishing and demeaning others is what we practice the most. It is indeed the selfish self-praise that vanity demands and that is but easily achieved by subjugating others. And thenceforth there we are; Demons in flesh and bone.

In order to achieve the noblest of states, one has to make selfless efforts for others and not for oneself. While we do efforts for ourselves and our families and that is essential and is a person's responsibility that cannot be evaded or avoided yet making efforts for others is but a challenge that faces mankind today and without this very effort, we cannot ever tame the devil inside. The first and foremost step in doing so is to love others and to love humanity without which no other effort may be made with heart and mind. If we help others for the sake of our praise, if we make any effort not for ourselves but for others with an ambition of personal or public recognition; we are doing nothing other than feeding vanity. This selfless effort is what can only be committed whence we love others in the first place. This indeed is the beauty that is so dear to God for he is the ultimate beauty Himself. When we love His creation, we praise Him and to Him all praise must be for He is the manifestation of all beauty in life and to Him we are to return. This very concept, the hidden truth about life, is so vividly put in the Quran (chapter Asr) that this does not remain but a hidden truth anymore for the one who looks upon it with an open eye. It is revealed in Chapter Asr that all mankind is in a loss save those who have faith, do the righteous deeds and in their mutual dealings and mutual relationships advice truth and patience. Those who have the real faith, the most unmoved, staunchly convicted faith in Him may do righteous deeds not powered by vanity but by love for Him, a love that is unconditional, immaculately absolute and eternal; and may promote and advice the real truth perhaps in better glorious happy days and advice patience and constancy during testing times and days of despair. However, all this has to be done selflessly and due to the pure love of God and not for vanity not for self-praise. This is most profoundly the purest and the most attractive beauty of a soul, the beauty that, in the words of the Prophet (SAWW), God loves. This is the knowledge that is given to man through imagination, observation and experience. The knowledge that God loves- the knowledge that is beautiful.

However, this does not stop here and this is not the climax. How can we forget that this is the end of another beginning only? Once we become beautiful we start searching for beauty itself. This is yet another journey. If we appreciate and comprehend beauty how can we ignore the one who created beauty and the one who is the most beautiful of all. If we love a creation how can we not love the creator? This is but not logical and rational. Therefore, all love leads us to Him; the God. We know him by different names do we not? Allah and His most beautiful ninety-nine names, God, Om, Khuda, Uper Wala, Elah are all but the names and attributes of only one God. Yes it is the same Allah who gives and forgives whereas we get and forget. According to Quran (Chapter 1 Verse 1) *"All praise is to God- the Cherisher and Sustainer of the worlds."* Hence by accepting that all praise is for Him, one denounces vanity and selfishness for only He is worthy of all praise. Everything is His and everything belongs to Him. He is the sole creator, nurisher, sustainer and cherisher of the universe. Therefore, all praise and love for beauty leads us to Him for He is the master creator of all beauty.

I understood, or may claim to have understood, no matter how little; the aforementioned concept with pain and agony through which I am going these days. But it is indeed good that I have realized, if not understood, this very concept without a misery greater than I could sustain, greater than I could comprehend before embracing insanity. As a young man during the days of my youth, I always had a few questions, the answers to some I am still finding, however the answer to one of them I have acquired through the knowledge that He bestowed upon me through imagination, observation and experience. It is indeed with age that I have understood the answer to this question, which I will reproduce hereunder. But this is the manner in which life teaches its disciples. Life, unlike the ordinary teacher, who would show the answers first and then take a test; teaches cruelly by taking a test first and then revealing the answers and that too only to those who have an open eye, an open heart and an open mind. This is how knowledge is attained. I always used to ponder and think as a young child and as a young man:

"If our loved ones are to die in front of us then why does God make us love them? Why does he not allow us not to love people only to the extent that their demise and final departure could possibly be fathomed by our heart and mind alike? If our loved ones are to die in front of us, God should not make us love them so dearly and so eagerly so that we could easily approve of their departure."

How incredibly difficult it is for a mother to see her child pass away. How unimaginably hard it is to bury one's father or mother. Or one's spouse or siblings or others one adores and holds near. This is one of the toughest realities of life that one has to go through in one way or another. If one has to do so by all means, then one should not love someone so dearly and so immensely that one sickens with the demise of a loved one. Things like the sickness or illness of your own children or that of your own parents for instance. How awfully and uncompromisingly and exceedingly unbelievable it is to see one's children in sickness and disease as well as to see one's parents aging through time and reaching an elderly stage, sick, feeble and decaying. God should not have made us love them in a manner of the like where everything becomes incomprehensibly unbearable. I had this question in mind. I had my imagination with me. However, my imagination was missing the other two tools that comprehend and develop knowledge. My observation ripened when I met Jibran's Prophet for it is indeed in such a poetic masterpiece that I found the meaning of the question and its answer that I was looking for. I was amazed that the question that has bothered me for so long must have also bothered Khalil Jibran. A long awaited surety that I wasn't on the road to folly. Jibran's Prophet revealed unto me: God makes us love our dear ones to the point of complete absoluteness that parting from them even for a day is difficult. Then He takes them away as they die in front of us only to let us know to whom in reality they did always belong to. In fact they were never ours in the first place. They never belonged to us. Indeed it is to Him that they belonged and in the end we all have to return to whom we belong, do we not? God makes us love and adore our dear ones selflessly and unconditionally and then takes them back to Him in order to teach us this lesson in a hard fashion that it is He who is the Master and not us in any case and He will take back what is His whenever and however He so desires.

And there we go shouting and crying and yelling about our possessions and belongings whether living or non-living, our egos and our esteems, our statuses and our positions. The concept of 'he is mine' and 'she is mine' has long eluded before my eyes. Everything is His and only His and hence to Him shall everything return. Witnessing the sickness of my children and the aging of my parents with my eyes was the last stage of my knowledge called experience that I was lacking and through that did I only comprehended the actuality of (Inna lillahi wa inna ilayhi raji'un) "Surely we belong to Allah and to Him shall we return."

Last but not the least; nevertheless, it is with this revelation that I can imagine a little, only a little, what befell Bhulleh Shah. What happened to him and what did he see and experience when he cried *(Tere ishq ne dera mere andar kita, bhar k zehr piyala main apey pita)* '*Falling in love with You was like taking a sip of poison.*' When he did that and indulged in such an ecstasy he further exclaimed *(Jhabde wahudi tabiba nahin te main mar gaiyaan)* "*Come my Healer, forsaken I am dying*' for this journey is not an easy one for the like of such great men whereas we, men of ordinary intellect, can merely understand the meaning of such things from the surface. And finally, whilst in his indulgence he cries for help and further dives in to the abyss stating *(Sanu ghayai kar k pher khabar na laiyan, Tere nachaya kar key thayya thayya)* "*you asked not once after you stabbed, your love has made me dance like mad.*"

It is with this reality that I now am able to have perhaps the little knowledge in understanding the answer to my question no matter how feeble such understanding is, for this quest took me from what is means to know to what it takes to know. Yet life did not give me the knowledge without its three phases, only to realise, what is the real essence of love and beauty in the eyes of God, as narrated in a singular moment, in a singular sentence by the wise Prophet (SAWW). The knowledge of an answer to one question only took me three decades of life whereas, along the way, I picked up a dozen questions more. My quest continues for the life of a knowledge seeker is a never-ending one. The hunger for more and longing and desire for knowledge, is, but a path crafted with illusion that shakes the very fabric of reality to a point where holding on to sanity is solely and essentially prudent. The knowledge, that to my naked eye, is made up of beauty and love, the very contrast between knowing that the known today may actually become unknown tomorrow in search of love, beauty and the Beautiful. Here I am floating, here I am swept away.

A Tale of Sheep and Lions

The greatest and the foremost fundamental human rights is the right to live freely. This has been derived from the notion that humans are born free and equal. Hence this is something divine and gifted to all homo-sapiens by nature and by virtue of merely being a human. God creates all humans as equals having their inherent right to life freely in this world. This is the reason why the very first article of the Universal Declaration of Human Rights postulates and I quote "All human beings are born free and equal in dignity and rights. They are endowed with reason and conscience and should act towards one another in a spirit of brotherhood." This is also something that almost every religion teaches its followers. Hence we now understand that the right to live freely is what is at the crux of human rights.

Contemporary world shows grave concern about human rights violations. Human trafficking is one of such evils, which have especially drawn attention of the western world because though the gravity of this evil nurtures in the east but disturbs the west on an enormous scale. Human trafficking more or less means "Obtaining, securing, selling, purchasing, recruiting, detaining, harbouring or receiving a person, notwithstanding his implicit or explicit consent, by the use of coercion, kidnapping, abduction, or by giving or receiving any payment or benefit, or sharing or receiving a share for such person's subsequent transportation out of or into a country or from one place to another within a country by any means whatsoever for any of the purposes mentioned above."

Human trafficking is supposed to be the third largest source of illegal income falling behind only the drugs and arms trafficking. Trafficked people are exploited in various ways including forced or cheap labour for agriculture work, domestic work, factory work, street hawking, but mainly for the sex industry while in the Middle East the ill-fated trafficked children are subjected to become camel jockeys to stir the camels in the races to run fast. Agony of the fact is that such stirring factor is none other than the screaming of the frightened little innocent child, which makes the camel run faster. The bidders of the race treat these miserable children just as fuel to pacify their barbarism. In the course of action, many children lose their lives or become disabled but fail to extract any sympathy from the stone hearts. Similarly every trafficked human suffers a lot at the hands of other human beings. People generally put themselves or their children in the hands of traffickers to escape poverty, discrimination or war etc. They are promised fantastic opportunities but find their selves tricked.

Some Facts

- One of today's biggest Human Rights crisis is international trafficking
- Third largest criminal industry only outnumbered by arms and drugs
- Fastest growing and profiting industry
- UN believes it generates $ 7 – 10 Billion annually
- 800,000 – 900,000 individuals trafficked each year; 80% are women and children
- It might become second largest criminal industry in the coming decade
- Costs are low (one time investment), high profits, constant supply and rising demand
- Unlike other HR violations, this is a global phenomenon. Happening all around the world today including Pakistan
- One country cant sort this out but since it's a global problem the whole international community needs to take part and act significantly against this evil
- Traffickers acquire their victims from poor third-world countries. The victims range from 5 to 18 years in age
- They are lured into stories of bright future normally as housemaids, restaurant server etc. in a wealthy country like UK, USA and Canada etc.
- Upon reaching the destination, their passports are taken away and they are forced in to prostitution and forced labour in factories etc.
- The cycle sometimes continues and they are trafficked to another country and re-sold for more profits
- Threats to border integrity
- Threats to human health: HIV/AIDS being transmitted to the victims, their clients and the families of their clients
- Threats to global human conscience, since slavery era

Localised View: Pakistan in transition

Pakistan is a **source, destination, and transit** country for men, women, and children trafficked for the purposes of sexual exploitation and involuntary servitude. Pakistani women and men migrate voluntarily to the Gulf, Iran, Turkey, and Greece for work as domestic servants or construction workers. Pakistan faces a significant *internal trafficking* problem reportedly involving thousands of women and children trafficked to settle debts and disputes or forced into sexual exploitation or domestic servitude. Unconfirmed estimates of Pakistani victims of bonded labor are in the millions. Women and children from Bangladesh, India, Burma, Afghanistan, Sri Lanka, Nepal, Azerbaijan, Iran, Kazakhstan, Kyrgz Republic, Turkmenistan, Uzbekistan, and Tajikistan are also trafficked to Pakistan for sexual exploitation and involuntary servitude. In addition, Bangladeshi, Sri Lankan, Nepali, and Burmese women are trafficked through Pakistan.

All the research reports so far conclude that trafficking in children is increasing at an alarming rate. However, in the absence of baseline data and because of its illusive nature, authentic statistics regarding the magnitude of the problem are not available. Estimation of the spread of the problem is further complicated by the fact that the crime often goes unreported and even if reported, there is lack of follow-up data regarding recovery and sometimes the incidents of missing children are not taken into account while dealing with trafficking. It is also difficult to estimate the span of criminal networks working in and outside the country. In Pakistan women and children are falling victim to trafficking mainly for the purpose of prostitution, sexual abuse, forced labour, camel jockeying, cheap labour, bonded labour, domestic servitude, selling of organs and marriage. In case of women and girls, the destination is usually the sex-market both within the country and outside. In the case of boys, the destination is usually Middle Eastern countries where they are engaged as camel jockeys. In most cases the girls, who are trafficked abroad, are trafficked to India, Malaysia, Indonesia and Europe etc. In case of the boys, Pakistan is usually treated as a country of transit to the Middle East. According to an estimate, there are about 700,000 trafficked Bengalis in Karachi today. People are trafficked from Pakistan on the pretext of fake marriages, for camel jockeying and through presenting them lucrative job opportunities. The main high risk areas are Swat and Mardan in

NWFP and Bahawalpur and Multan in Punjab provinces. Mostly, the people trafficked from Pakistan are sent to the Middle East whereas a very small proportion ends up in Europe. Men are also trafficked, however, the issue of trafficked men is almost absent in the literature on trafficking in Pakistan. So far men are predominantly seen as "migrants" while women and children are typically seen as being "victims of trafficking" reflecting a strong gender bias in mainstream literature on trafficking. There is no proper asylum procedures in place and that is the reason why all the trafficked people who come in to Pakistan and detained at the borders, if caught, and then deported back to their countries. The biggest and the foremost dilemma here is that the authorities still see the victims as accused. The victims of human trafficking are sent to jails and have to go through the agony, which is only suitable for the accused and not for the victims. There is no such policy or mechanism to deal with the trafficked victims, let alone rehabilitation efforts. It is estimated that each year thousands of Pakistani people are deported back to Pakistan. Only last year there are around 1,300 Pakistanis deported back to Pakistan from Ukraine, Turkey and Greece.

I therefore stress on the fact that the new paradigm of thinking on trafficking in Pakistan should recognize the phenomenon of trafficking identify distinctions and interface between trafficking and migration and indicate the need for analysing the concept of trafficking both from the supply and demand sides. The most important element to be considered here is the fact that the government is unable and unwilling to improve the overall situation. There is no political wisdom and/or will to incorporate the international norms and laws in to Pakistani legislation in order to meet the requirements of curbing such an evil form the country. According to my observations and findings FIA officers cannot even differentiate between "smuggling" and "trafficking". The Government of Pakistan does not fully comply with the minimum standards for the elimination of trafficking. However human trafficking has been criminalized through the enactment of the Prevention and Control of Human Trafficking Ordinance 2002, yet there has been less work done than the expected. This ordinance was promulgated in lieu of the passport Act. According to FIA, there have been 1700 arrests but not a single conviction is reported. There is a weak implementation of the ordinance. Most of the FIA staff is even not aware of Human Trafficking due to the reason that there is no training and no sensitization. Apart from that, there have been 700 officers of the FIA nominated and trained on human trafficking in order to combat this evil. However, these officers do not possess adequate training and/or understanding of the concept of human trafficking. There is only one national academy of FIA in Islamabad and the course that they offer to officers surprisingly does not include any module on human trafficking. Another very important factor is that the concept of internal trafficking is not even being considered by the authorities. The trafficking Ordinance only covers international or external trafficking however internal trafficking remains unnoticed.

What to do? Suggestions

- Improve border security mechanism which if could be brought near to leak proof can be a great success in tackling the trafficking issue;
- Training FIA for adoption of more advanced mechanism and techniques; thereby strengthening the asylum regime
- Use media for the spread of awareness and knock at the conscience of people;
- Ensure the presence of reliable process to trace the trails of trafficking and involve the government agencies to cooperate and reach down to the source;
- Help installing the scientific checks on the monitoring of the Trafficking in Persons (TiP) by integrating the civil society, NGOs and the government officials under one umbrella.

The most important action that needs to be taken if one is really committed to curb this evil from the country is to raise awareness of the masses and in particular that of the NGOs and CBOs i.e. the civil society. Particularly of those NGOs that are working directly against human trafficking. In connection with the above, there is a dire need to train the relevant authorities on investigation methods and procedures so that their capacities are raised up to a level where they can perform to their best abilities in not comprehending the phenomena but also working pro-actively against such an organized crime in the country and can also in this way collaborate with international agencies working to curb this evil. Hence, after the completion of the aforementioned two parts of this grand recommendation, a unique **task force** could be established wherein the actors could be comprised of an even bench of both the civil society and the relevant authorities who can monitor the trafficking activities within the country as well as try to persuade and indulge the required political will within the concerned government machinery.

Pakistan remains in deep problems originating from trafficking in persons. Both the concerned government authorities as well as the members of the civil society need to work collectively as a singular unit to resolve these problems. This mafia has to be stopped otherwise our children and youth will remain a victim of this evil called human trafficking; a crime as heinous as none other. Many people intend to go out of homes in search of earning their bread and butter however at times they are caught in this net innocently. The authorities need to look upon these people as victims and not as offenders; these people do not know of what happens to them once they get caught in this evil, they become slaves for their entire lives. Human trafficking, in my opinion, is the biggest violation of human rights. The biggest right is the right to live freely and trafficking takes that divine right away from people caught up in this menace by one way or another. People are exploited, either knowingly or unknowingly, due to poverty and fall victims of this menace. This has become a multimillion dollar industry; a crime that is expected to outnumber trafficking of arms and drugs. This is rather alarming and astonishing. Whether known to the victims or not; this still is a violation of their basic and fundamental human rights and therefore needs to be stopped. We can all stop this menace either by taking necessary steps to stop trafficking or else inducing measures to promote and safeguard migration practices. Both of these are inversely proportional to each other however for a country as badly caught in this as Pakistan both of these areas need to be worked upon simultaneously; without which we will not be able to help our younger generations.

Women are a vulnerable segment of this society and if we look at the number of women being trafficked to or from Pakistan renders them more vulnerable at the mercy of the organised trafficker's networks. Unless their rights as workers and the right to migration are not protected, they will keep on falling in this most horrendous dilemma of all times. We do not live in the Roman slavery era today and therefore we need to concentrate on our efforts to make this for real by promoting safe migration practices to curb human trafficking.

There is felt a dire need for Pakistan to work hard against this menace in order to secure the future of our children and that of our children's children. It is indeed true that poverty, unemployment, migration and urbanization are the underplaying causes of human trafficking but it is never enough to attribute these to be the causes and do nothing else. It will take time in eliminating poverty, unemployment and other social problems but we cannot wait for that to happen first and allow, in the process, our youth to be exploited yet we all need to nib the evil in the bud by raising awareness on these lines particularly in high risk areas and generally all across our rural and urban parts of the country.

The Green Glory

What the 2011 Cricket World Cup is to me for Pakistan is exactly what the 1995 Rugby World Cup must have been to Nelson Mandela for South Africa. This is the only living hope and pride for Pakistani unity- the only event where I see Muslim, Hindu, Sikh, Christian, Sindhi, Punjabi, Pathan, Balochi Kashmiri and others abroad flamboyantly rejoicing and enchanting Pakistan Zindabad. This will be our finest hour- this will be our moment of greatness: *The Green Glory!* It does take a lot of courage and determination to do what the Pakistan cricket team is striving to establish. Without forgetting the tireless efforts of Waqar Younis, the man who is leading the team from the front is obviously Shahid Afridi. Nature is truly an astonishing and complex phenomenon. Who could have expected that the highly criticised cricketer Afridi could turn the tables and unite all the boys under his unified command well supported by Younis. Afridi is leading the team from the front no doubt and is doing wonders. The level of engagement of Imran Khan in this world cup and this highly anticipated Indo-Pak semi-final says it all. Imran Khan, who is now a politician, perhaps also saw the green glory and is hence supporting more than ever before, the green shirts. He is perhaps having glimpses of his own times and knows very well what it means for Pakistan to win a world cup amid terrorism and extremism driven western paranoia about Pakistan.

Africa's Afridi

Mandela saw after getting released from prison and holding office that even though his struggle for Apartheid has borne fruit, yet he knew that the tribal and racial differences in South Africa would not easily end. There was violence and fighting everywhere between the Blacks and the Whites. However, Mandela knew that there is only one thing that binds his nation truly and that is Rugby and hence he inspired the whole nation as well as the team to win the World Cup and bring all South Africans together under the flag. Every particle of the universe assisted him in this just cause and he was able to unite South Africans after enabling his team through his inspiration to win the world cup- not for them but for the nation. That was his greatness and reward. After that cup the world saw a different South Africa. Mandela met the team captain and inspired him by relating to him what he sees in the world cup and how he envisions the world cup trophy paving the way for a better and united South Africa.

His vision was shared by the South African rugby team Springbok's Captain Francois Pienaar, without whose understanding Mandela had no other option. The Captain had difficulty in making his boys understand the same however he did not give up hope and transpired into the team, with the help of Mandela himself, what had to be achieved. Mandela had seen and knew what wonders Rugby can do for the scattered and shattered South African nation. He did that in a way none other could have done that by enabling the team to win the World Cup for the country. During the World Cup all the blacks and whites waved the flag together and embraced each other because Mandela had involved them, through the game of Rugby, to come close to each other and understand that the racial difference is only in their eyes and not in the eyes of nature. Once done, all the tribes and people of the nation united under one flag and hence the day the world cup was won by South Africa- Apartheid was literally dismantled from within South Africa. The country and nation that we see today is exactly the miracle of the century and Mandela deserves a place, in my heart, high above all other 21st century leaders. In my opinion, nature wanted Mandela to succeed and that is why she helped Mandela win the world cup otherwise no matter how inspiring he might have been; if he was not a true man of cause, the world cup might never have been won. Therefore, winning the world cup for South Africa was a godsend. Mandela proved himself by ridding the African society of Apartheid that he had a soul unconquerable- that he had a soul dispossessed!

Cricket Diplomacy; an incidental chance

Dr Manmohan Singh, the Indian premiere and to me a man of great regard and esteem, has invited PM Gilani because he clearly saw an incidence of cricket diplomacy in the semi-final. Dr Singh did not really invite Gilani to see the match but to talk on bilateral interests. Gilani announced today that there will be no talk on Kashmir and Kashmir is off agenda for this visit. This, I believe, is a good move given that the major bone of contention between India and Pakistan is Kashmir and has the capabilities of derailing the bilateral processes. Secondly, if the government is appeasing and bowing to the US interests in Pakistan already, our neighbours may also deserve some room in it. This has come amid a time when dialogue between the two countries is underway. I do not have high hopes from this venture but then one can never understand how natures moves, as she moves in a mysterious way. I expect that the two countries can forward friendship and have relations like US and Canada for it is the only way forward. Dr Singh is a big Indo-Pak friendship promoter but has been under huge pressure of the Indian right wing politicians. Let us see if this match can bear fruit and melt the ice or not. This is another important dynamic that the game of cricket has for the two countries.

Glorified Unification

Nonetheless, Pakistan does not seem to have a Mandela here but Rehman Malik who warned the team recently to beware of match fixing as he has a close watchful eye on them and that they might even be under surveillance. I am not comparing for comparing Mandela to Malik would be worse than committing suicide for me. It is just a hint at how people perceive things. Imran Khan's statement was an answer to his remarks when he said maybe it is Malik who should be watched and monitored. This leaves us to rely on the only leader of the day; Shahid Afridi who was once a criticised cricketer but is now a major source of pride for the nation. I have been absolutely amazed to note that the Indo-Pak semi-final has the power to bring all Pakistanis together; something that no leader has been able to accomplish. Now what does that mean? It simply means that the Pakistani nation is striving for GREATNESS and for GLORY. The political leadership has failed the test of winning the hearts and mind of its people in Pakistan and that is a fact. As a result the Pakistani nation is becoming faithless and hopeless and hence has become an easy prey to racial discrimination, social evils, moral vacuums and sectarian violence. Today the Pakistani nation exhibits the properties of a crowd and not that of a nation. During these times, when I see all the people of Pakistan irrespective of their cast, creed, colour, gender, age, regional identities and religion attempting to unite under the Pakistani flag- I clearly see that my nation strives for greatness, glory and unification. We do not have greatness in us today and that is something this world cup trophy can bring to Pakistan, as it did to the South Africans one and a half decade ago. However, it will depend on the fact that Pakistan should win the world cup and by winning the world cup I mean defeating India in the semi-final because that is our world cup. And if

Afridi can bring the trophy back home again he will be able to inspire the nation towards that greatness that they long for.

I was once a cricket player myself and a great fan of Pakistani cricket, however, I gave up my interest when I could no longer hear on the radio "Over the wicket comes Wasim Akram from the Pavilion end, bowls to Sachin Tendulkar, he nicks it away to the keeper, he is out! He has been taken by an in-swinging surprise..." and it is only now at this time that I seem to be involved deeply into cricket once again like the good old days.

It is only because of the fact that I long for greatness in my country and hence would like to see the homecoming of the Green Glory.

The Rise of the Self

This essay is an academic paper written with intensions of expanding the knowledge of "Iqbaliyat" to the common reader. Through this paper, I will endeavour to explore the basics of Dr Allama Iqbal's philosophy of the Self (Khudi). However, this philosophy is so huge a concept and so immense a reality that it can only be fully explored after diving in to its depth along with Dr Iqbal. Hence putting light on all areas of his lifelong work revolving around the human self or ego would not be possible here. Therefore, I will attempt to highlight the very basics of this philosophy, to which Dr Iqbal had devoted his full life, in order to interpret, the best that I could; the true essence of the philosophy of self.

Attempting to take on a subject like this is already a difficult intervention. Similarly, when I started to think about structuring this paper in a way that renders it openly understandable to the common reader, I was face to face with a great complexity. But since I had decided to put some light on the subject under discussion, I proceeded to construct this paper in three parts in a way that it will first explore the actual source of his philosophy including a discussion on the true meaning of his source and then afterwards present an elaboration of what the philosophy of self means in actual reality and, in conclusion, highlight the human reformation process that he talks about. This paper will include discussion from theological, religious, social and philosophical perspectives, without which I believe developing a true understanding of "Khudi" is not possible. I find it pertinent to comment here that through this attempt, the reader will be able to understand, apart from the source and meaning of the source of the philosophy; Dr Iqbal's philosophy of self all together in a nutshell and also the process of the refinement of his own "Self" or "Khudi" in the light of "Iqbaliyat."

The Source

Iqbal never spoke of the source of his philosophy in public for a very long time even though that he was criticised by some to have simply followed the works of others by taking inspiration from philosophers like Neitzsche, Kant, Goethe and Bergson in the west and Rumi, Saadi and Ghazali in the East. Although Iqbal never denied taking inspiration from their works as a student of philosophy yet his philosophy, as a practical poet-philosopher was widely misunderstood in this relation. If we closely examine his work, we easily find it unique in its essence and entirely different from the works of his predecessors. The true source of his inspiration for the generation of his philosophy of self was narrated publicly by Syed Nazir Niazi (a close companion).

The Historical Dialogue: Syed Nazeer Niazi said that he once asked Allama Iqbal that "Some say that your philosophy of self is taken from Bergson or Neitzsche while some relate it to the works of other philosophers. Why don't you say for yourself as to what is the actual source of your philosophy of self." Dr Iqbal said "All right you should come visit me tomorrow and I will dictate it to you." Nazir Niazi says that he got delighted for being so fortunate that the poet of the East, the Orator of the nation will dictate the source of his philosophy to him. So he went to him the next day, excited, with his notebook. Iqbal asked him to bring the Quran from the bookshelf. At this moment all my excitement was taken aback, says Nazir Niazi, because I had thought he would tell me something from the history of philosophy, he will refer to some other philosophers etc. but he just made me bring the Quran. When I brought the Quran he asked me to recite only one single verse from it, which was from the Chapter "Al-Hashr (The Exile)" and it was verse 19, which read **"And be not like those who forgot Allah (became disobedient to Allah), and He caused them to forget their own selves. Such are the rebellious transgressors."** After reading it aloud, I looked up at him, perplexed; he was smiling, and he said "This is it."

The aforementioned dialogue tells us that Dr Iqbal had taken the inspiration for his philosophy from a single verse of the holy Quran. Therefore, in order to comprehend this philosophy, we will have to first understand the true meaning of this verse from which Iqbal took his inspiration and then embarked on a philosophical and spiritual journey that ended in the generation of a new philosophy. According to the verse, simply put, Allah says to the people that they should not be like those people who forget Him because if that happens to be the case then Allah, as a result, makes them forget themselves, since those people are the ones who are rebellious and go, in such a rebellion, beyond the limits and boundaries of the religion and sanity. Now what does Allah intend to teach us all here? He is warning all mankind that if we do not follow Him or otherwise forget Him, then we will forget ourselves; or that we will forget our "Self". Forgetting self could have two possible forms i.e. (i) forgetting the physical self and (ii) forgetting the spiritual self. Here in this verse, the indication cannot be towards the physical self or bodily life because one will never forget to dress up, eat, comb one's hair etc. Therefore, Allah is referring towards the spiritual self. Hence the question arises as to what is a spiritual self, which is but easy to understand. The physical self relates to the physical abode or earth whereas the spiritual self relates to the spiritual abode or the heavens. This point can also be proven in a metaphysical sense by arguing that while a person dies the physical self remains here and is buried to decay whereas the spiritual self is taken back to the Creator to live on. This in turn means that the spiritual self being referred in the aforementioned verse is none other than one's own spirit or ego or "Khudi" or self or precisely put *the Soul*. Hence in this verse Allah is saying that those who forget Him and His commandments are bound to be made to forget their inner-egos or souls. Moreover, as we know that our bodies, made up of matter, and did not come from above but were made down here by a biological process however our souls are not a biological process but those are the divine energy resource breathed in to our bodies by the Creator himself, which is the very reason why he is called Al-Khaliq (the Creator). Hence Allah relates directly to our souls in that verse and warns those who transgress that He will make them forget their souls or otherwise make them spiritless. This reference of spiritlessness is further elaborated by Dr Iqbal and he concludes that spiritlessness is not the absences of spirit, which is never possible given that spirit is in the continuous state of being, but it is the stagnation of spirit and such stagnation occurs when one transgresses from the divine word of Allah.

A question may be crossing the mind of the anxious reader here that since the spirit or the soul has descended from above or by Allah then why must there be those who tend to forget Allah. Why do sinners commit sin? Why is the being not absolute? Why did Allah not make the soul believe in Him, if He breathed it in to the human in the first place? These are only a few metaphysical questions that one keeps asking oneself. In fact, Iqbal puts some light on this concept better than nobody else could ever do. Let us then examine this in the light of his teachings in order to understand the true essence of the verse of Quran (59:19) under discussion. Iqbal argues that knowledge is a continuous process. This also means that knowledge was always there but man's thought remains limited and hence his knowledge remains limited till the time he starts to gain knowledge through two things in particular i.e. his own thought and imagination as well as his practical experience. Since the soul knows no death and was even alive before entering its physical abode on earth i.e. the human body; then why is it that the soul has forgotten everything to which it had the knowledge in the heavens? Iqbal then takes on to explain this philosophical question in such a manner that was not known to the human mind ever before. He talks about this in detail in one of his lectures delivered at the Mardas, Hyderabad and Aligarh namely "The Reconstruction of Religious Thought in Islam." He contests and I quote *"Adam was forbidden to taste the fruit of this tree obviously because his finitude as a self, his sense-equipment, and his intellectual faculties were, on the whole, attuned to a different type of knowledge, i.e. the type of knowledge which necessitates the toil of patient observation and admits only of slow accumulation. Satan, however, persuaded him to eat the forbidden fruit of occult knowledge and Adam yielded, not because he was elementally wicked, but because being 'hasty' by nature he sought a short cut to knowledge. The only way to correct this tendency was to place him in an environment which, however painful, was better suited to the unfolding of his intellectual faculties. Thus Adam's insertion into a painful physical environment was not meant as a punishment; it was meant rather to defeat the object of Satan who, as an enemy of man, diplomatically tried to keep him ignorant of the joy of perpetual growth and expansion. But the life of a finite ego in an obstructing environment depends on the perpetual expansion of knowledge based on actual experience. And the experience of a finite ego to whom several possibilities are open expands only by method of trial and error. Therefore, error which may be described as a kind of intellectual evil is an indispensable factor in the building up of experience."*

It is evident from this excerpt that Adam (PBUH) ate the fruit from the tree of knowledge just because Satan convinced him that rather than waiting for a long time and allowing the natural process of knowledge development and intellectual growth, he would gain the absolute knowledge in a shortcut. Hence when Adam ate the fruit thereby disobeying Allah, he had to be sent to earth and since earth is not a place as good and pure as heaven therefore his self or soul had to be made low in order to allow him to tune in to the toil and pain he would have to undertake in order to survive on earth. Henceforth the soul was made to start from the scratch, that is to say, it was not allowed anymore the knowledge it had gained before. Thereafter began a process of evolution wherein the soul develops and gains expansion in terms of becoming the kind of an intellectual faculty that progresses in attaining knowledge over time. This discussion is sufficient to provide concrete evidence of the fact that Allah is addressing the transgressors in the Quran (59:19) and is saying that if you transgress Allah will let you astray in a sense that He will make you forget your soul or "Self."

I would just take a moment here to explain the "Fall of Adam" in order to complete our understanding of the source and meaning of Iqbal's philosophy of self. The fall of Adam is explained in full in the Quran (Ta-ha: Chapter 20 verses 115-123) according to which Adam was banished from the heaven for eating from the tree of occult knowledge, or better still, as Quran puts it, when Satan seduced both Adam and Eve by whispering to them that he can lead them to the tree of knowledge that leads to the "kingdom that never faileth" (Mumtaz Mufti calls it the state of the Ultimate Now). Hence they ate and their nakedness became visible to them and they covered their nakedness with the leaves. Thereafter Allah banished them from heaven and sent them down to earth thereby lowering their Khudi or self or ego or spirit or soul to a level suitable to their abode, the earth. Hence the soul was blinded from the knowledge known to it before and it had to start from the scratch. This is why Allah refers to make one forget one's self if one disobeys. Similarly, in the same chapter verse 124 Allah says ""But whosoever turns away from My Message, verily for him is a life narrowed down, and We shall raise him up blind on the Day of Judgment." Now this again does not mean that those people will be blinded physically by taking their eyes off; but it means that their souls or Khudi would be blinded because they had forgotten Allah's message and hence would be in a state of spiritlessness and devil will be their partner. Hence the reference of this verse puts more light on the fact that Allah is referring to the self or the human ego or soul, which is all that is there in this universe and in the hereafter encompasses the soul. If we can purify our soul, we will go to heaven if not we will go to hell; this is the ultimate test and this is the meaning of the source of Iqbal's philosophy of the self (Khudi). I gather that if you have read all of the above with interest the meaning of Iqbal's most famous verse *'Khudi ko ker buland itna ke her taqdeer se pehle ... Khuda bande se khud puchey bata teri raza kia hai"* would have become clearer to you in its true essence.

The meaning

Throughout his works in both poetry and prose, Iqbal's message revolves around 'Khudi' and the rise of the self. He teaches the concepts of the rising of the self to the Muslims of the Indo-Pak in his mission to try to revive their souls so that they could get back on their feet, understand the level of their destiny, of Adam and of heaven and ultimately of Allah. Iqbal relates and concludes, at times, that if a person starts to work on his self or soul and tries to purify it, it will always lead him to Allah because Allah is the source and the energy to which one's soul is attached. Therefore, he argues that the philosophy of self is better understood when one realises that this world is but a test of the purification of the soul and in that purification one finds one's true connection to Allah; one's Creator. He obtains the view that love is the entirety, there is nothing in this world but love and the more one purifies the soul the more one becomes accustomed to love and at the highest level, everything vanishes but the love for Allah succeeds and remains forever because we are talking about the soul that cannot die with our earthly death and reaches out to Allah in the afterlife, so if that soul upon our worldly death is full of love for Allah; just imagine that the challenge has been undertaken. The point of reference here is that the human heart is the only place where one can store this love and hence the heart is the place where Allah is; hence we have to purify our hearts not only to keep our love stored there but also to find Allah in the same heart. This process deals with, in the beginning, self-actualisation leading to self-realization. Therefore, purifying one's heart is the first step towards raising one's Khudi or soul or self to a level where one can easily see Allah with the eye of the heart. Once the heart is pure, one literally starts to see Allah in oneself.

Dr Iqbal has many a times argued that the difference in western and Muslim philosophers is just this factor that the western philosophy ends at the refinement of the human being or better still the search of the better being however Muslim philosophy ends at the refinement of the human being to find Allah or in the search of Allah. He further explains this by stating that since everything is love hence it also has to have an end and that end has to be beauty. Hence the end for all love is beauty. Here Iqbal refers to love as the soul or self and the end of the self as the beauty or Allah because nothing in this world is more beautiful than Allah. Life, to him, is a continuous river; without an end. There was life, in another form, before the life on earth and there will be life after the earthly life so life is a flowing river, which has no beginning and no end or in other words it is the beginning of the end of another beginning. Therefore the spirit has to evolve and keep moving and that can only occur when spirit is attached to the fabric of hope. Hopelessness is spiritlessness where spiritlessness is not the absence of spirit but the stagnation of spirit and those who will have spiritlessness will be made blind by Allah of the day of the reckoning, as explained above. Therefore, there is no room for hopelessness and I gather this is the very logic that is attached to the fact that suicide is not allowable in Islam because suicide is caused mainly due to hopelessness or spiritlessness. The philosophy of self hence teaches us to become the masters of our own destinies. To shape our life on this planet and even beyond by shaping the soul so that when it travels back to its Creator; it carries the fragrance of the love of Allah and nothing else. This is the rise of the self, this is the rise of Khudi.

Conclusion

Iqbal does not only talk about the rise of Khudi or self in his philosophical endeavours but also reveals the process of human development. The process of such a development that leads or causes the Khudi to rise above to a level that is required for a person to attain a degree of self-consciousness before God when his destiny is given in his hands and nothing is then beyond his reach. Do not be surprised to know that this is the stage that Adam attained when he ate from the tree of occult knowledge that was bound to lead him to the gardens of the "kingdom that never faileth" or to a state of the ultimate now (where the sun never sets). I believe that the actual concept of Khudi has now been properly expressed to a level understandable to the common reader of this paper. Therefore, last but not the least, I will finally put some light on the process of the development or the rise of the self, as Iqbal puts it. As it is now understood that the rise of the self would mean the rise of the soul and that will be done in the first place by the purification of the heart in order to pave the way or clean the home in which the love has to reside. This love will give rise to the self to the level required to get to the beauty, which is God Almighty. Iqbal highlights a three step process for the rise of the self, explained in brief hereunder:

1. Obedience to the divine law
2. Self-Control (highest form of self-consciousness)
3. Divine Vice-regency

This means that there are three steps that one needs to undertake in order to enable one's Khudi or self to rise above. In the first place one has to accept the divine law or the Oneness of God (Tauhid) and remain far away from indulging in seeing God in plurality (Shirk). This is also the very first step, of the purification of the heart, according to the Islamic faith. When one attains this stage then comes the next phase, which is maintaining a high level of self-control. This is a practice that the Sufis had mastered. It is true that when one possesses absolute self-control, one gets the devil scared away and eluded and the reason is that devil needs to break one's self control in order to pollute one's heart and soul. Therefore, when one practices the divine law and has self-control the devil is defeated. Similarly in the last phase comes the divine vice-regency. We have been made the vice regents of Allah on this earth and it is our duty to share love and mercy with our fellow beings. Now a question is that how one can attain this divine vice-regency of God? Well the answer to this is way simpler than one could think. To obtain the divine vice-regency one has to do nothing except practically adopt the message contained in Quran (Al-Asr chapter 103). This chapter is translated as " By (the Token of) Time (through the ages), Verily Man is in loss, Except such as have Faith, and do righteous deeds, and (join together) in the mutual teaching of Truth, and of Patience and Constancy." Hence doing this allows man to obtain the vice-regency of God. These are simple four things namely having Faith, doing the righteous deeds, preaching truth and patience. Nevertheless, this chapter reveals all the three stages as well. Stage one is narrated here as having faith, stage two as doing the righteous and preaching the truth and patience. Finally, I wish to conclude that the human race, Muslims and Non-Muslims alike, require to adopt this three phase strategy revealed by Dr Iqbal in order to secure the noblest state before God and attain peace and tranquillity in this world as well as in the hereafter. May God Almighty allow us enough strength and courage to do the needful. I have developed this academic paper out of my love for Dr Allama Iqbal in order to expand and disseminate his message on one hand whereas, in my efforts to try to bring Iqbal back in our lives on the other. I have tried to the best of my capabilities, my thought, my knowledge, my observations and experience as well as understanding of Iqbal to put proper light on the true essence of the concept of Iqbal's philosophy of the self in a way that should touch the heart of the reader, provide logic and belief to hold on to; in this chaotic world that we live in and remove the obstacles in understanding the word of a man, who, as his philosophy teacher Arnold puts it, "is a man for his age and is a man ahead of his age."

About the Author

Q. M. Sidd is a development professional and has served in the past with the United Nations for different agencies including the UNHCR and UNESCO in different capacities. Right now he is working as a CEO and founding member for an independent development organization, Inspire Pakistan in Islamabad, Pakistan. Moreover, he has also remained a trainer on Human Rights for the Pakistan Police, the Federal Investigation Agency, legal fraternity, judiciary and other government and private institutions. Furthermore, he has been a Consultant for various development organisations.

An MBA and Master of International Relations (Foreign Affairs) degree holder he has also remained an Associate Professor on the subject of International Human Rights Law and United Nations, for the International Islamic University and Islamabad School of Law.

This book "A Dance in Melancholy" is the first volume 'Homebound' of the series and is a collection of his articles, essays and memoirs written over a period of five years. While he continues to write articles and memoirs and shall publish another book in the series at the appropriate juncture, he has been writing short stories and is working on his first novel. The short stories shall be published as a collection in the due course of time.

He mostly writes on Philosophy, Spirituality and Mysticism, Current and International Affairs, Human Rights and Social Development under non-fiction whereas under fiction, his short stories and the novel being written have a dramatised philosophical undertone.

He records his weblogs on www.theorthodox.wordpress.com

www.ingramcontent.com/pod-product-compliance
Lightning Source LLC
Chambersburg PA
CBHW070820290526
45795CB00002B/777